McCall Collection of Modern Art

The American Scene— Early Twentieth Century

by EMILY WASSERMAN

Published by Fratelli Fabbri Editori,
Publishers, Milan, Italy, and

The McCall Publishing Company
New York, New York

American Art at the Turn of the Century

In the early 1900s it would have been farfetched to believe that within fifty years a distinctly American art would be accepted and admired by an international audience. That any strictly native style would eventually establish itself and its leadership over Europe's modern movements would have seemed even more incredible. Although many of the country's nineteenth-century artists, such as George Catlin, Winslow Homer, and Thomas Eakins, as well as the Hudson River landscape painters like Thomas Cole and Frederick Church, had gained international prominence for their visions of continental splendor or their views of the nation's customs and inhabitants, it was not until the twentieth century that a national consciousness in art began to emerge and establish itself.

It was an era in which immigration from eastern Europe, Ireland, and Italy was heaviest, making the coastal cities great melting pots of cheap labor for industry, which was growing at a fantastic rate. Women began their fight for suffrage rights. Legislation for labor and social welfare was being enacted. During such a period of upheaval and socio-economic reorganization, art was hardly one of the country's chief products.

Furthermore, American artists were still dominated and often trained by the academies of Europe, as well as by the rules of their own academies in the United States, although these national institutions never could claim the power and influence of their European counterparts. American collectors favored second-hand imitations of Barbizon School landscapes, watered-down Impressionist copies, or pseudo-French salon-studio Realism. Official tastes neglected the experimental artists, and economic support was denied those who wanted to try something new and different.

As industrialization and technology developed with increasing speed during the early twentieth century, so too did art. But it took many years of experimentation, complicated by constant vacillation between allegiances to the traditional art of the European masters on the one hand, and a chauvinistic reliance on patriotic or regional and genre subject matter on the other, before American artists could distill their efforts into an art worthy of serious consideration. America's art did not fully mature to an independent expression until after World War II.

Robert Henri and the Eight

The first officially organized group of twentieth-century artists dedicated to the development of a style expressive of the American experience was known as The Eight, and later as the Ashcan School of New York Realists. The group included William Glackens, John Sloan, George Luks, Everett Shinn, Ernest Lawson, Maurice Prendergast, and Arthur B. Davies, the eighth being Henri himself. Particularly concerned with the variety of urban life, a number of these men began their careers as newspaper illustrators. Such men as Henri, the guiding spirit of this revolution against academic control of style, teaching, and the rights of exhibition, are notable in the history of American Art less for their own painting than for their crusade against elitism and traditionalism. His liberal attitudes and teaching encouraged a democratic, humanistic approach to art, and he inspired a generation of younger artists to break away from the rigid aesthetic formulas of organizations such as the National Academy. Henri and his group effected a vital rift with the methods and rules of that tradition in the name of democratic individualism in art. However, they did not emphasize the production of art for its own sake, nor did they advocate an art of didactic, socio-political, or experimental significance. Instead, they sought to incorporate their art with what they knew and observed of life around them. All considered, their work was conservative.

At the Pennsylvania Academy, Henri had been a student of Thomas Anschutz, who, in turn, had been the protégé of Thomas Eakins. Although Eakins had stirred that institution with his nude life-drawing classes and his spurning of academic teaching techniques, his art, like that of The Eight, was still conventionally based on the realistic observation of nature and life.

When Henri studied in Paris in 1888, and a decade later when he returned there, he submitted work to the official Salon rather than to the more progressive Salon des Indépendants. In favor of realistic action and expressive subject matter portrayed through dynamic brushwork and flashy surface effects, Henri rejected the more advanced European moderns like Monet, Cézanne, and Renoir. Instead, he chose the older European masters whose work he had observed while in Paris: Goya, Velázquez, Hals, and (more modernly) the early Manet —all of whom he admired less for their radical approaches to form or space than for the more superficial aspects of manner, such as surface highlights, bravura painterly treatment, and spontaneous characterization of types. Henri's paintings of the period reflect a talent for sharp observation of worker-peasants, society ladies, Spanish dancers, gypsies, immigrant children (*Laughing Child*, 1907), and various street scenes. His greater achievement, however, seems to have been his magnetic personality and the charismatic manner in which he instructed his students and colleagues during informal studio gatherings at the New York School of Art (William Merritt Chase School) in 1904, and later when he opened his own school. His students at the latter included Glenn Coleman, Guy Pène du Bois, Rockwell Kent, George Wesley Bellows, Edward Hopper, Stanton MacDonald-Wright, Patrick Henry Bruce, Stuart Davis, Kenneth Hayes Miller, and Yasuo Kuniyoshi, some of whom were to be the accomplished artists of the next generation.

The only real connection between the members of The Eight was their mutual commitment to the principle of artistic nonconformity. Their actual styles varied greatly. Although Sloan, Glackens, Shinn, and Luks all had done illustrations for Philadelphia newspapers, contact with Henri converted them

2

to oil painting. Rejected by the National Academy, these painters, who had moved to New York from Philadelphia, organized and held their own exhibition in 1908 at the Macbeth Gallery. The showing prompted critics to label them the "apostles of ugliness"; some work was sold, however. Lawson (*High Bridge*, 1934) and Prendergast (*The Promenade*, 1913) painted in modified Impressionist or Neo-Impressionist styles, Davies portrayed romantic, dreamy idylls recalling the nineteenth-century French-Classical painter Puvis de Chavannes, while Henri, Luks (*Hester Street*, 1905), Shinn, and Sloan (*Sunday, Girls Drying their Hair*, 1912) dealt with the urban street; Glackens, like Prendergast, was occupied with happier, more bourgeois themes of parks and promenades. Although Shinn also favored the glitter of the music and dance halls (*Revue*, 1908), Henri's colleagues tried to deal with European modernism. Sloan looked to Cézanne for more solid structure, Glackens turned to Renoir and Manet, and Prendergast kept up with the Neo-Impressionist movement, Seurat, and Cézanne, but their works remained rather conventional nevertheless.

A little-noticed but encouraging event occurred at the same time as the Macbeth Exhibition of The Eight. Around 1908 the wealthy sculptress Gertrude Vanderbilt Whitney opened her MacDougal Alley studio to those young artists who wanted to get together and discuss their work away from the academic milieu. A friend of both Henri and Davies, she helped in backing the Independent Artists Exhibition and, in 1918, she formed the Whitney Studio Club, where exhibitions were held for antiacademic artists Sloan and Hopper, and sculptors such as Reuben Nakian and John B. Flannagan. The function of the club, which was expanded in 1930 to become the Whitney Museum on Eighth Street, was to persuade the reluctant public to purchase the work of young American artists. Her support was vital for many struggling painters and sculptors, and the recognition from exhibits and her patronage was invaluable at a time when few critics approved of American innovations.

In 1910, Henri, his friends, and students set up the unjuried Spring Independents Exhibition in New York, giving the younger artists a chance to show their work. Large crowds testified to the successful initiation of the artists' rebellion, but critics were still negative. This rebellion did establish new goals for American Art and encouraged greater tolerance for the direct, the eccentric, and the individualistic. Artists were no longer forced to look to established prototypes for authority, although European models would not be completely overthrown until the 1940s. Nevertheless, Henri and his colleagues had created a favorable climate for the broadening of the bases by which art in America could be created and judged. Although he was not an aesthete or an intellectual, his teachings offered a middle road attractive to many young artists.

The Armory Show

Confirmation of Henri's artistic revolution was not long delayed. In 1913, the Armory Show, or more properly the International Exhibition of Modern Art, was held at the Sixty-ninth Regiment Armory in New York. The plan was to exhibit painting and sculpture, incorporating both Europe and America's most representative contemporary artists. It combined Henri's democratic ideal with gallery-owner Stieglitz's avant-garde notions of uncompromising experimentation and artistic independence, proclaiming "the new spirit in art" for the twentieth century.

Artists—not dealers, academy officials, or professional museum administrators—were the initiators and organizers of this vast enterprise. Advised and accompanied by expatriate painter and critic Walter Pach, artists Arthur B. Davies and Walt Kuhn barnstormed Europe from Cologne to Paris, collecting material for the European section of the show. Pach helped them locate works by Picasso, Duchamp, and Braque, while American painter Alfred Maurer, in Paris at the time, introduced the envoys to the Impressionist dealer Ambroise Vollard, who dispatched many major contributions. Although the two ambitious organizers aimed for a broad scope and liberal viewpoint, many limitations of the final show resulted from the shortcomings and predilections of their taste. In spite of these obvious pitfalls, however, the products of the artistic revolution that had been brewing quietly under the auspices of Stieglitz in the back rooms of his 291 Gallery (also called the Photo-Secession Gallery) were finally aired.

There is probably no single event that has had as much impact on the development of American Art as the Armory Show. It stimulated outraged public opinion, to be sure, and it also affected the evolution of style and created a new, broader market for collectors of both American and foreign art. A new class of art patrons developed in contrast to the previous century's millionaire barons such as Henry Clay Frick, J. P. Morgan, and Andrew Mellon, who had cared only for prestige collections of Oriental and European antiquities, old masters, or earlier American Art. This new breed of collectors, dedicated to the cause of Modern Art, was composed of professional men like lawyers John Quinn and Arthur Jerome Eddy, crusading socialites Lillie Bliss and Katherine Dreier, and moderately well-off people concerned with the acquisition of art as educational material for an uninformed public, not merely for its immediate aesthetic appeal or its value as an investment.

The exhibition was circulated to Chicago, where it confronted critics and the public with the significant transformations that had occurred in Europe during the previous half-century.

The Armory Show was actually divided into two sections—the American and the European sections. The American division featured works by the men who organized the show. It also contained paintings by more traditional Realist and conservative painters, all somewhat embarrassingly surpassed by the more radical achievements of Europe's Impressionist, Post-Impressionist, Fauvist, and Cubist artists, as well as by their nineteenth-century predecessors. America's younger, more courageous artists, The Eight, or Stieglitz's circle, most of

4

whom had traveled or studied in Europe, still had not fully absorbed the formal or conceptual advances made on the Continent.

Works by Matisse were numerous, reflecting Kuhn's preference and the basis of his own later style (*Musical Clown*, 1938). Davies was responsible for the Symbolist paintings of Odilon Redon, whose affinity to the American's obscure reveries is distantly apparent. Canvases by Cézanne, Braque, Picasso, and Marcel Duchamp's then infamous *Nude Descending a Staircase* were also exhibited in the predominantly French European division.

Sculpture was poorly selected, with only a few examples by Rodin, Maillol, Brancusi, and Lehmbruck as tokens. The genre paintings of The Eight and of men like Guy Pène du Bois looked a bit old-fashioned next to works by their colleagues Patrick Henry Bruce, Arthur B. Carles, Max Weber, Alfred Maurer, Andrew Dasburg, John Marin, Abraham Walkowitz, Morgan Russell, Stanton MacDonald-Wright, or even Maurice Prendergast, who at least had begun to take the European trends and ideas into account.

But the cultural and aesthetic gap between the two continents was obvious even in the more adventuresome American examples. The display of Cubism and other new movements was to provide a stimulating model for American artists during the next decades. In the years immediately following the great exhibition, native practitioners of abstraction were few, however. It was not until the late thirties and forties that American artists were to find their independence in that area.

Critical and public response to the show was unfavorable and outraged. The more narrow-minded critics decreed that the Europeans were simply charlatans, dubbing Duchamp's *Nude Descending a Staircase,* for example, "an explosion in a shingle factory." Conservative writers denounced the anarchic heresy of the modern painters. A more open-minded critic sensed the importance of the exhibition yet confessed that the work was difficult to grasp.

In an era when American Art suffered from lack of vital contact with the European avant-garde spirit and the foundations of artistic exploration, the nation was entering a period of political isolation in reaction to the waves of immigration from the Old World. A defensive position about the country's art was connected with a feeling of threat about alien invasion of the national culture. A hostile public with a backlog of prejudice in moral, ethical, and cultural matters was not going to accept a new art out of hand. America's taste in art has customarily leaned toward direct expression, technical accomplishment, didactic or illustrative pictures, and forms uncomplicated to the eye and understanding. Cubist or nonobjective styles were bound to be rejected in the face of such attitudes.

Many of the attacks elicited by the Armory Show confused cultural, political, and moral issues with those more pertinently raised by the radical art styles. Accepted criteria formerly applied to academic or realistic painting could no longer be used for the analytic methods of Cézanne or the Cubists, nor could they enlighten the viewer about the expressionistic distortions of Gauguin, Van Gogh, Kandinsky, Matisse, and the Fauvists. Moralistic epithets were used by the critics to support their personal indignation and to hide the lack of intelligent comprehension of an art that had now moved beyond their doctrinaire understanding. The show, however, did force a new awareness of an exciting, living tradition upon American artists, making them come to terms with their own independence. Contemporary, indigenous art could no longer be ignored, and though it took several more decades to overcome the neglect and ridicule to which American artists had been subjected, many positive effects began to be felt.

Museums still neither purchased nor showed native experiments in modernism, and only cautiously accommodated the European precedents, while private collectors acquired the best of this work. Scientist Dr. Albert C. Barnes from Pennsylvania, Lillie P. Bliss, lawyers John Quinn and Arthur Jerome Eddy, literary connoisseur Walter Arensberg, two sisters, Dr. Claribel and Miss Etta Cone, artist Albert E. Gallatin, educator Katherine Dreier, midwesterner Ferdinand Howald, and some persons of relatively moderate means, gathered the finest paintings and sculptures from Europe and America. Art schools took longer to update, while some of these new collectors took the educational burden upon themselves, giving lectures, circulating exhibitions, and later donating their collections to public institutions or galleries. Many of these people were advised by the artists who fostered the Armory Show, rather than by dealers. Davies, Kuhn, Duchamp, and Glackens were all instrumental in the formation of fine personal collections, as well as in advising many new galleries that opened in the wake of the show.

William Glackens, whose own art was, to a large extent, dependent on the Impressionism of Renoir's impressionistic work, had hopes that an indigenous art would be stimulated by the Armory Show. He admitted our dependence on the French, but was optimistic about the development of a "truly national art." In order to revitalize the nation's art, artists, as well as the public and the critics, had to overcome a mistrust of extremism, and combine a new openness with the already well-developed American penchant for experimentalism.

Before the signal year of 1913, many American artists had served apprenticeships in the art schools and studios of Paris, Germany, or Italy. The influence of the European avant-garde began to filter back through the enthusiastic response of these painters who witnessed the rise of Cubism in France and kept track of the other movements that developed there in the early years of the twentieth century. In fact, the artists in America who were committed to a modernistic approach could not deny the necessity of revamping their approach and their style of painting or sculpture after the great event of 1913; many of them were forced to reevaluate the forms and reorganize the structure of their work.

Although many artists visited Europe and returned with the will to test what the innovators were developing on the Continent, their attempts were often inept or approximate. One of the few supporters to whom these artists could turn was Stieglitz, a pioneer in the field of photography — which he maintained was an independently valid, aesthetic medium, equal in status to painting or sculpture. Stieglitz championed the cause of Modern Art through his financial backing of many younger American artists and expatriates, his galleries in New York, his patronage of European artists, his exhibitions of their work in the United States, and through publication of magazines such as *291* and *Camera Work* (1902–17). These were high-quality documents of the photography, aesthetic theory, and experimental literature and criticism of the period.

Stieglitz was as devoted to the European moderns he promoted (Brancusi, Cézanne, Rodin, Matisse, Picasso) as he was to his special protégés at home (abstractionist Georgia O'Keeffe, who later became his wife, Hartley, Maurer, Oscar Bluemner, Charles Sheeler, and the struggling sculptors Gaston Lachaise and Elie Nadelman). This internationalism and favoritism were very much in keeping with his esoteric attitudes and elite tastes; he stood for artistic isolation and individualism, experimentation for the cause of "art for art's sake" and not for social significance. Stieglitz also understood the artists' problems in relation to an unsympathetic audience, but he refused to reconcile the artist with that public. He was often unwilling to explain the sense or purpose of the art he exhibited to uninformed potential customers. What he exhibited and endorsed was for the consumption of a small and enlightened minority.

In spite of his professional prejudices and personal eccentricities, Stieglitz did introduce superior examples of radical art from Europe and original work of Americans at his various galleries. From 1905 to 1911 he ran the 291 Gallery on Fifth Avenue in New York; in 1916 he joined in the organization of the Forum Exhibition at the Anderson Galleries in New York. This was an attempt to make up for the disappointing American entries at the Armory Show. From 1925 to 1929 he organized shows at the Intimate Gallery housed by the Anderson Galleries, and from 1929 to 1934 at An American Place. Stieglitz encouraged many who would not otherwise have had the chance to exhibit or the occasion to be recognized. He and his coterie of artists, photographers (Edward Steichen, Paul Strand), critics and writers (Sadakichi Hartmann, Marius de Zayas, Gertrude Stein), and committed customers were among the first to articulate the modernist styles in America. He perpetuated the idea that the modern artist should think of himself as a member of a small, very special group, whose creativity and work need not give in to popular tastes or to the demands of the market. He is, therefore, considered one of the foremost historical figures of the early twentieth century — a dealer, tastemaker, aesthetician, photographer, and patron. The lessons of experimentation and productive, courageous radicalism that Stieglitz fostered were to come hard to the public. But it is undeniable that his influence forms the keystone of that education, setting standards of high quality in art.

American Cubism, Precisionism, and Synchronism

World War I virtually severed artistic relations between America and Europe. Cultural interchange and patronage was interrupted by problems of social and political urgency, though most artists tended to be pacifist. Visual propaganda was left to the commercial designers and illustrators, while American painters continued in their efforts to consolidate the issues detonated by the Armory Show. Artists like Guy Pène du Bois (*Morning, Paris Café*, 1926) and Kenneth Hayes Miller (*Shopper*, 1928) made awkward syntheses of the formal disciplines suggested by post-Cézanne or Cubist painting and their own eclectic versions of Realism based on contemporary subjects. Any attempt to employ the Cubist vocabulary or methods was bound to look like a provincial imitation — and, indeed, most American artists who fashioned themselves as Cubists understood only the rudimentary surface effects of the style. Naturally, because Cubism was the sensation of the Armory Show, it was destined to become a fad in the hands of commercializers. The decorative style of handicrafts, architectural ornament, and graphic illustration known as the 1930s "moderne" or "art deco" was (at its worst) the ultimate result of the degeneration of Cubism in the hands of those who considered it a novelty.

O'Keeffe, Hartley, Dove, Marin, and Maurer, to name a few, continued to pursue their convictions about the validity of emotional response to aesthetic content and subjective material. The more rigorous phase of analytical Cubism represented by the 1910–14 works of Picasso, Gris, and Braque made little discernible impression on the majority of Americans. It may be that, because Cubist ideas were promoted in America by some of the style's minor stars — Duchamp, Francis Picabia, and Albert Gleizes — when they visited or settled in New York shortly after the Armory Show, native imitators did not even base their works on the finest examples of Cubism. Painters like Preston Dickinson maintained a stiff interpretation of Cézanne-like composition in tonally subdued representations of American industrial or rural complexes. Italian Futurism seemed to offer an inspiration to Max Weber and Joseph Stella, who both looked to the dynamic movement and splintered, animated drama of the Italians' urban epics. Man Ray was one of the few to have crystallized a genuinely Synthetic-Cubist manner (*Five Figures*, 1914), but his activity as a painter was brief. He later turned to Dadaist objects and photographic experiments like his sprayed "aerographs" or his delicate "rayograph" portraits and abstractions made with sensitized photographic plates.

Perhaps the intellectual austerity and perceptual analysis demanded by the classic phase of early Cubism was simply not in keeping with America's artistic preference for the realistic or the lyrical. It was to the coloristic branch of

Cubism, headed by Frenchman Robert Delaunay and called "Orphism" by poet André Breton, that the most programmatic group of American Cubists turned. Synchronism, as this short-lived movement called itself, was essentially the product of two painters who had studied and worked in Paris, becoming acquainted with current scientific color theories and with the work of Delaunay and friends (*Synchromy* was the name of one of the founder's paintings and meant "with color.") Stanton MacDonald-Wright and Morgan Russell declared their intentions in a manifesto published on the occasion of their joint exhibitions held in Munich and in Paris, both in 1913. They wanted to paint with areas of distinct spectrum color that would be blended only in the viewer's eye, evoking rich-colored volumes. Nevertheless, their first exhibited paintings —still lifes and figurative studies—fell short of this ideal. Russell returned to figurative art, alternating afterward between that and abstraction, and Mac-Donald-Wright also moved away from Synchronist experiments.

Synchronism certainly predicted the major concern with color painting that would mark the more wholistic, single-image chromatic art of the later fifties and sixties. But after its short, temporary existence, little was done to extend or enlarge its findings. Patrick Bruce was one of the few to develop a significant personal idiom out of this experience, but he burned most of his work from the twenties before he committed suicide in Paris in 1936.

The Dadaist activity that centured around the home of Arensberg was often produced to scandalize a public too self-satisfied or uninterested to pay attention to serious artists. While the group that collected to applaud this activity sponsored eccentric performances of music, published liberated writings, and created anarchistic paintings or constructions, they did induce a more favorable climate for artists to consider the most extreme forms of experimentation as valid means of creativity. Conventional formulas could be challenged and new boundaries established, but there were just as many artists who preferred to rescind their wild, youthful forays into the avant-garde as those who chose to risk its freedom. Men like Charles Burchfield or Thomas Hart Benton looked back on their work (now obliterated) of the twenties with distaste and embarrassment. For this reason, a completely accurate visual record of this period is difficult to establish.

Some works of the Surrealists are also related in mood to the paintings produced by the group in America known as the Precisionists or "Immaculates." Impersonal, seemingly timeless images, unpopulated by humans or other incidental details, were the mark of this movement. Included in this loosely organized group were such painters as Charles Sheeler, Charles Demuth, Rawlston Crawford, George Ault, Niles Spencer, Peter Blume, Joseph Stella, Stuart Davis, and Preston Dickinson. Taking off from the sardonic treatment of machine themes by Duchamp (*The Bride*, 1912), Schamberg, and Picabia, these painters set about diagraming the lucid structures of the American farm and industrial landscape. Their styles tended to idealize structural simplicity

9

and clarity of design. These artists sought more banal themes, through which they aimed to portray the geometric order inherent in the country's anonymous and functional architecture.

Basically conservative and moderate as a phenomenon, classical in spirit though regionalist in intent, the Precisionists' work counteracted the more topical and illustrative anecdotes of American Scene painting turned out by the more rurally focused painters like Benton, Curry, Burchfield, and, later, by Andrew Wyeth (*Perpetual Care,* 1961) in the forties to the sixties. Less ambitious and provocative than Synchronism, Precisionism was, at least, not the eclectic compromise of illustration and academicism that American Scene painting proved to be. It sought a viable basis for an American tradition and found it in the utilitarian contemporary landscape.

The Thirties: Grass-roots Tradition, Social Protest, Magic Realism, and Abstraction

The crisis in national and cultural identity precipitated by the Depression had a decisive effect upon the emerging generation of American artists. Some felt the need to idealize virtues and sermonize traditional values of the rural, Puritan-Calvinist, independent American farmer or worker in a society where rural types and their way of life were rapidly being subsumed by the spread and complexity of urban life. Nostalgia appealed to that sector of the public that feared the loss of small-town rural life or the relinquishment of its political isolationism. The paintings of those who followed in Henri's tradition were most popular in this context. American Scene artists counted Thomas Hart Benton, John Steuart Curry, Grant Wood, and, nominally, Charles Burchfield among their number. Their urban counterparts included painters like Reginald Marsh, Raphael Soyer, Jerome Myers, Paul Cadmus, Kenneth Hayes Miller, Isabel Bishop, and Yasuo Kuniyoshi, and others who had studied with Henri and now perpetuated their viewpoint at the Art Students League in New York. Social consciousness was the banner that united most of these artists. Provincialism in style as well as subject matter—corn fields, churches and farms, working girls, and city derelicts—became the stamp of a national art. Traditional illusionism and stylization were the techniques most favored to express these scenes and views.

Benton, Wood, and Curry virtually rebelled against the consequences of modernism introduced to American artists by the Armory Show, while another more independent Realist painter, Edward Hopper, was able to utilize the lessons of abstraction in his haunting psychological investigations of the American mentality and environment.

As the tenor of political and economic life became ever more oppressive during the thirties, with poverty and unemployment hitting new highs, another group of artists chose to retreat from reality. These men, the Magic Realists, characteristically relied upon personal, imaginative fantasy, projected into pictorial form by means of illusionistic or excruciatingly detailed realism. The Americans who practiced some version of this style—Ivan Albright, Peter Blume, Louis Gugliemi, Alton Pickens, Philip Evergood, Morris Graves, Edwin Dickinson—chose commonplace imagery and transformed it by dreamlike illusions, mystical speculation, or intricate techniques. Meanwhile, figurative painting continued as a familiar and accepted idiom, though often taking the form of social protest, and later veering toward expressive abstraction, as in the work of Milton Avery, Arshile Gorky, and Willem de Kooning. Many artists were active in leftist or socialist politics during the thirties, while others simply campaigned for basic human rights.

At the opposite pole from Hopper, the Regionalists, and the Social Protest artists was Stuart Davis. Like many of his contempories, he too had been a student of Henri's and his development parallels the period of Hopper's career. Davis was virtually the only artist ambitious enough to reconcile the premises of Cubist abstraction with the more localized American Scene painting. Davis could not adhere to a unilateral evolution. He was profoundly affected by the Armory Show and was openly critical of Henri's failure to repudiate academicism completely or to substitute for it a truly new kind of art and purpose. Davis labored through the crudities of his own early work in order to assimilate the advanced notions and radical implications of French art into a refined and clearly American idiom. Similar to the Precisionists, Davis looked for formal patterns in everyday objects, and, as he became more aware of planes and their spatial relations, he developed his first real series of abstractions, the "Eggbeater" pictures of the thirties. Late in the decade Davis painted several large murals under government auspices. Deeply involved with the texture of the American experience, like Hopper and the other Realists, Davis more boldly changed the forms of that context to suit his own artistic needs and to fulfill the goals of advanced modernist painting (*Eggbeater V,* 1930).

Later Thirties and Early Forties: The War Years

In the thirties, the threat of oncoming war, joblessness, and the closing down of the luxury market for art caused many artists to swing back to "an art for the proletariat." Although economic and spiritual depression made artists realize the necessity for organized activity, it was government support that finally catalyzed the country's painters into a self-conscious group. In the decade between 1933 and 1943, the single most important factor for the maintenance and future of art was the patronage of the federal government providing known and unknown artists with commissions, monthly stipends, and materials. Artists were employed to decorate municipal buildings, banks, post offices, housing projects, schools, railroad stations, or public edifices as part of the Public Works Administration initiated by President Roosevelt's New Deal. Although much of the work turned out under the projects now appears stylisti-

11

cally irrelevant, the major achievement was the quantitative fact of artistic production during such difficult times. No less important was that cultural awareness was stimulated by an extensive effort to foster art appreciation through teaching, art tours, the establishment of Federal Galleries and Community Art centers, traveling exhibitions, and museum lectures. Another important result of this organizing of artists was that a valuable audience of peers was provided by the artists themselves; figurative painters were exposed to and met the small band of abstract painters, and dissension among stylistically opposing factions was minimized.

Abstract art did not offer any viable answers to the nation's social or political problems. The political right among artists and public favored American Scene/Regionalist painting, sentimentally dreaming that home cures constituted solutions for those dilemmas, while the political left advocated an art of emphatic social protest. Abstract artists also tended toward the left.

Like an earlier generation who had been to Europe to work and study there about the time of the Armory Show, many of the abstract painters gained contact with the Europeans from apprenticeships in France, since the United States was not yet a major refuge for those who fled Hitler. Although Holty, John Graham, Gorky, de Kooning, and others had been born in Europe, their painting was not affected by such origins. Charles Shaw, Morris, Albert E. Gallatin, John Ferren, and Carl Holty were the fortunate Americans of the period who either lived in Paris for long periods or visited the city frequently, so that they were important bearers of knowledge about new developments there. John Graham brought enthusiasm for Picasso and Abstract Art in general back to his friends Gorky, de Kooning, and David Smith, publishing his record of their thinking and his defenses in a prophetic but didactic book entitled *The System and Dialectics of Art* (1937). Morris's writings, Diller's knowledge of Mondrian and the Constructivists, and Gallatin's important collection of Abstract Art exhibited at his Museum of Living Art in Washington Square after 1927 were also vital channels for Americans to learn about the leaders of the abstract mode.

In 1936 the Museum of Modern Art held its Cubism and Abstract Art show directed by Alfred Barr. No Americans were included because of space limitations. The museum avoided becoming a center for the activity of native artists because Barr declined to support them, maintaining that their work was not original or distinctive. Although the Whitney Museum's only show of this type in 1935, Abstract Painting in America, did incorporate several native artists— Browne, Gorky, Shanker, Knaths, Pereira—it too played a negative role. In 1937 the Solomon R. Guggenheim Museum of Nonobjective Art was opened, where Kandinsky's free lyrical abstractions were on view. The New York artists, however, were not on the best of terms with its director, the Baroness Hilda Rebay, so the museum's facilities were of slight benefit to them. Showcases did exist, nevertheless, in the form of many private galleries.

12

Gradually, with the intensification of conflicts in Europe, artists fled to New York, their presence constituting a vital stimulus during the forties. The influx of masters from Germany, France, and Holland meant direct contact with personalities and living ideas rather than a reliance on reproductions or second-hand accounts from those who had been abroad. Although the length of time spent here by these men varied, short visits by Jean Hélion in the mid-thirties, by Léger in the later thirties, and by Piet Mondrian during the forties did stimulate a new awareness of abstract principles. Purist Hélion argued for the correspondence between the nonrepresentational flat or modeled forms that he used and the equally abstract thinking of the scientific, technological age. Léger's bold mechanical forms and powerful women or workers spoke with similar relevance to the American experience. Josef Albers (*The Gate,* 1936) had taught art at the Bauhaus in Dessau, Germany, before he emigrated to the United States in the early thirties. His major contribution was in the field of art education, teaching at Black Mountain College for thirty years, a center and laboratory for radical activities, where many important future leaders of art, criticism, music, architecture, and design attended. De Kooning, Franz Kline, Robert Motherwell, John Cage, Buckminster Fuller, Clement Greenberg, and others were among those who would mold the art and aesthetic principles of the fifties and sixties.

Hans Hofmann, who had taught in Munich (1915–32) before coming to America, instructed at the Art Students League until he opened his own New York school in 1934. Hofmann did not exhibit until 1937 or again until 1944 and he never showed his work to his students. Hofmann's teaching concentrated on the opposition of colors and planes suspended in space, on positive-negative antitheses of energy and movement, and on his well-known theory of compositional tension, the "push-pull" principle. This meant that the oppositions set up within a picture could be resolved or balanced by the degrees to which intensive color, dynamic lines, or expressionistic paint application were emphasized or suppressed (*Effervescence,* 1941, or *Spring,* 1940). Surface and depth would then operate simultaneously as contrasting visual factors.

While the majority of those who exhibited with the A. A. A. were adherents of the Purist/Constructivist/Neo-Plasticist persuasion, another group of artists took Picasso as their chief model. Lee Krasner, who later became Pollock's wife, (*Untitled Abstraction,* 1939), de Kooning (*Study for W.P.A. Williamsburg Housing Project,* 1935, and *Elegy,* 1939), Gorky (*Garden in Sochi,* 1941), and John Graham were among those who followed Picasso's manner, with its surrealized spacing of partly biomorphic, partly geometric, black-outlined forms. Graham, older than his friends Gorky and de Kooning, was in some ways closer in his thinking to Hofmann. Graham was a Russian counterrevolutionary who had escaped to America in 1920 and had later made many trips to Paris. As a connoisseur and collector, particularly of African Art, and as an aesthetician, he influenced his associates through his veneration of Picasso and his condemnation of the Social

13

Realists who, according to his view, had failed to concern themselves properly with revolutionary aesthetic values. Graham anticipated the evolution of art and thinking in later decades with certain of his stylistic and theoretical predictions, and as early as 1937 to 1941, through his endorsement of artists like Pollock, Avery, David Smith, and Gorky before their talents had matured. His first purely abstract paintings of the thirties were destroyed. He later turned against Picasso and sought for his models in the classical masters. He painted "copies" of these old masters in the form of strange, hypnotic portraits of women, disturbingly juxtaposed with arcane and magical symbols drawn from astrology, alchemy, and numerology, reflecting his interest in psychoanalysis and the art of primitive tribes (*Two Sisters*, 1944). Although he too eventually renounced abstraction *per se*, Graham benefited from, and stimulated his colleagues in, the forms of primitive art and the workings of the unconscious as sources of creativity. He served as an important evangelist for the cause of Abstract Art and for the revolution of forms and methods necessary to its independence.

An American Art Emerges

It is interesting that Graham's friend Gorky was claimed by André Breton, the poet-spokesman for Surrealism, as one of the only Americans acceptable to that movement. Gorky is thus considered to have straddled the period between Hofmann and Graham's generations, and the first of the Abstract Expressionists who was to dominate the painting of the later forties and early fifties in America.

Contact with the Surrealist techniques of automatically allowing images to flow from inner fantasy into realized pictorial form provided Gorky with a ready means to transcribe the richness and range of his own imagination and memory. *The Liver Is the Cock's Comb* (1944), painted not long before his suicide in 1947, is a welter of brilliantly tinted forms that evoke pieces of landscape and anatomical fragments floating in a disruptive dream state. Nature was one of his most frequent points of departure, and Gorky fused generalized natural forms with subjected motifs drawn from memories of childhood, from images of sexuality, and from the vocabulary of geometric abstraction. He worked from careful preparatory drawings, filling in with color while expanding and rearranging on canvas. His emotional metamorphosis was toward a more agonized style, dissolving the visceral, delineated forms in a surreal space. This method of burying configuration in a sea of painterly strokes and improvisations was paralleled in the subsequent work of his closest friend, Willem de Kooning, and it also serves as the connection between Gorky and his heirs, the Abstract Expressionists. This pictorial legacy was taken up and further developed in the works of Pollock, Philip Guston, Bradley Walker Tomlin (*Burial*, 1943), James Brooks, Franz Kline, Adolph Gottlieb, Barnett Newman,

14

Clifford Still, Mark Tobey (*Cirque d'hiver*, 1933), Mark Rothko, William Baziotes, and Conrad Marca-Relli.

De Kooning was not at all interested in the Surrealists, though his superb draftsmanship allied him to Graham and Gorky's passionate interest in the old masters. During the thirties, de Kooning painted many muted, poetic portraits (*Man*, 1939), as well as articulate pastel-hued, Picasso-like abstractions. Like Gorky, his interpretation of Cubism's dynamics was rather free. He dealt primarily with the theme of the human figure, developing over several decades a series of *Woman* paintings (*Pink Lady*, 1944) in which the female form was successively submerged, then reemerged in an ambiguous spatial environment swept with the frenzied strokes of a heavily loaded house painter's brush. Although the surface looked brutalized, colors were often the same chalky pinks, corals, pale greens, and grays or tans used during the thirties. This gestural flux, with its contradictions, revisions, and discontinuities between figure and ground or representation and abstraction, was the basis for more entirely abstract works—many done solely in black and white during the forties, and including some of his finest work.

Contours and patchlike jagged or curving shapes take over the role formerly played by the figure with a viscous, allover calligraphic fabric in these paintings. This would be further explored and refined by Pollock in his own later muralized (*Mural* for Peggy Guggenheim, 1943) and elegant, masterful "drip" paintings of the mid-forties. Increased painterliness, dense, rough texturing, and an unfussy approach to techniques and to forms, which progressively dissolved the notion of referential content, became the mark of a distinctly American style of painting during the next decade. Factions polarized around these two artists, de Kooning and Pollock, just as the camps had split between two other aesthetic leaders, Henri and Stieglitz, earlier in the century. Like Henri, de Kooning, solidly grounded in old master draftsmanship and the European tradition of modernism, looked back to the authority of precedents as the basis of a new style; Pollock, the restless young innovator, was concerned, like Stieglitz, with the radical implications of his work and thinking for the future of avant-garde art.

Artists in New York who were part of the same aesthetic milieu and generation as de Kooning and Gorky soon began to dispense with configuration altogether, concentrating fully on the dramatic, subjective qualities of the painted gesture. A larger scale, perhaps encouraged by the mural painting under the W.P.A., became more and more common and had the effect of confronting the viewer with an overpowering directness, encompassing him with the raw dimensions of the artist's emotional and formal experience.

After an early phase in which a number of these "first generation" Abstract Expressionists—Pollock, Newman, Still, Rothko (*Omen of the Eagle*, 1944), Gottlieb, Baziotes, and Theodoros Stamos—employed subject matter based upon ancient classical myths and primitive symbols invoking the aura of crea-

15

tion and elemental life, or borrowing emblems from the realms of the universal, collective unconscious, an abstract, "action-generated" style dominated. This kind of symbolic content was expressed quite differently from the Surrealists' interest in similar themes. It was an effort to break away from both European-based abstraction and what several of these artists had complained was the stigma of American Scene painting, Social Realism, academic prizewinners, or the generally trite work that appealed to the general public and to most "established" museums as well. In order to reassert the artist's connection with the fundamental richness and primordial nature of the human imagination and its creative spirit, such content seemed temporarily necessary so that national history and personal biography could be transcended, since true symbols of contemporary life, relevant to the aims of advanced art, were difficult to discover in the work that confronted these men historically. Their later paintings, which appeared to be so far from human experience in their increasing reductiveness and distilled abstractness, were nevertheless profoundly concerned with the maintenance of the heroic, humanistic tradition.

There was nothing impersonal in the painterly handwriting of these giant canvases, which were the spontaneous record of an artist's sensibility responding self-confidently and with a newfound relevance to the tensions, values, and context of the American experience.

Thus, the first truly authentic native painting style was achieved during the period immediately following World War II. Contacts with the teaching of the European avant-garde and with its expatriates have provided a vital link with models, principles, and personalities of importance. American artists were still a long way from the international, or even national, recognition that they deserved. It would be a decade more before this startling, expressionistic new art would be understood or accepted. But the break had been effected, and the way had thus been paved for the fulfillment of the dream of an independent, innovative, and modernist American form of art—an art that Henri, Stieglitz, and the pioneers of the Armory Show generation had nurtured in the face of discouraging odds during the early decades of the twentieth century.

PLATES

The Ashcan School and the Realists

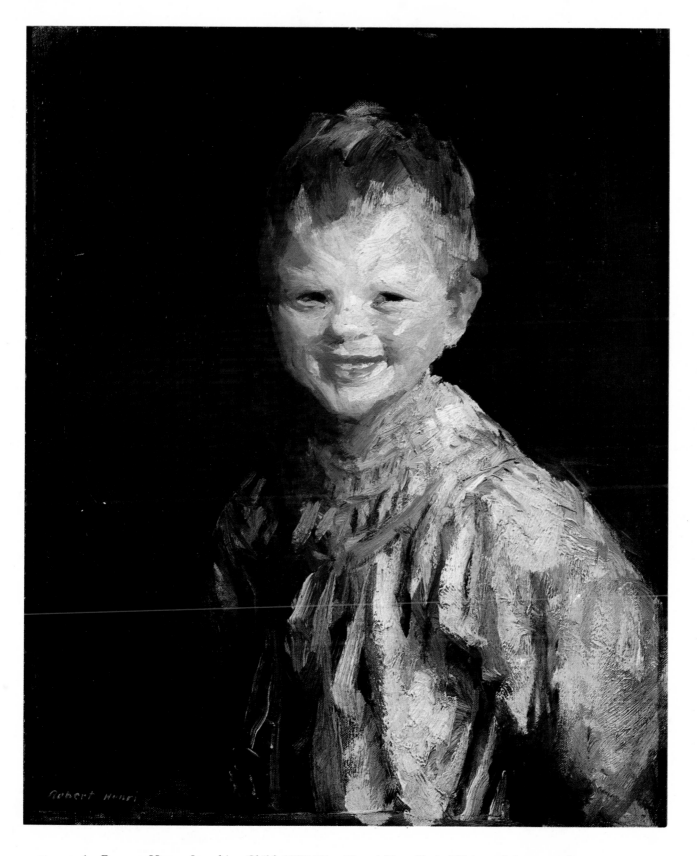

PLATE 1 ROBERT HENRI *Laughing Child*, 1907 (61 x 51 cm) New York, Whitney Museum of American Art

PLATE 2 WILLIAM GLACKENS *Nude with Apple,* 1910 (102 x 145 cm) New York, Brooklyn Museum (Dick S. Ramsay Fund)

PLATE 3 JOHN SLOAN *Sixth Avenue Elevated at Third Street,* 1928 (76 x 102 cm) New York, Whitney Museum of American Art (Photo: Sandak)

PLATE 4 GEORGE BELLOWS *Dempsey and Firpo*, 1924 (130 x 161 cm) New York, Whitney Museum of American Art

PLATE 5 George Luks *Hester Street*, 1905 (66 x 91 cm) New York, Brooklyn Museum

23

PLATE 6   ERNEST LAWSON *Winter on the River,* 1907 (84 x 102 cm) New York, Whitney Museum of American Art
(Photo: Sandak)

The Stieglitz-291 Group

PLATE 7 JOHN MARIN *Region of Brooklyn Bridge Fantasy,* 1932 (48 x 57 cm) New York, Whitney Museum of American Art

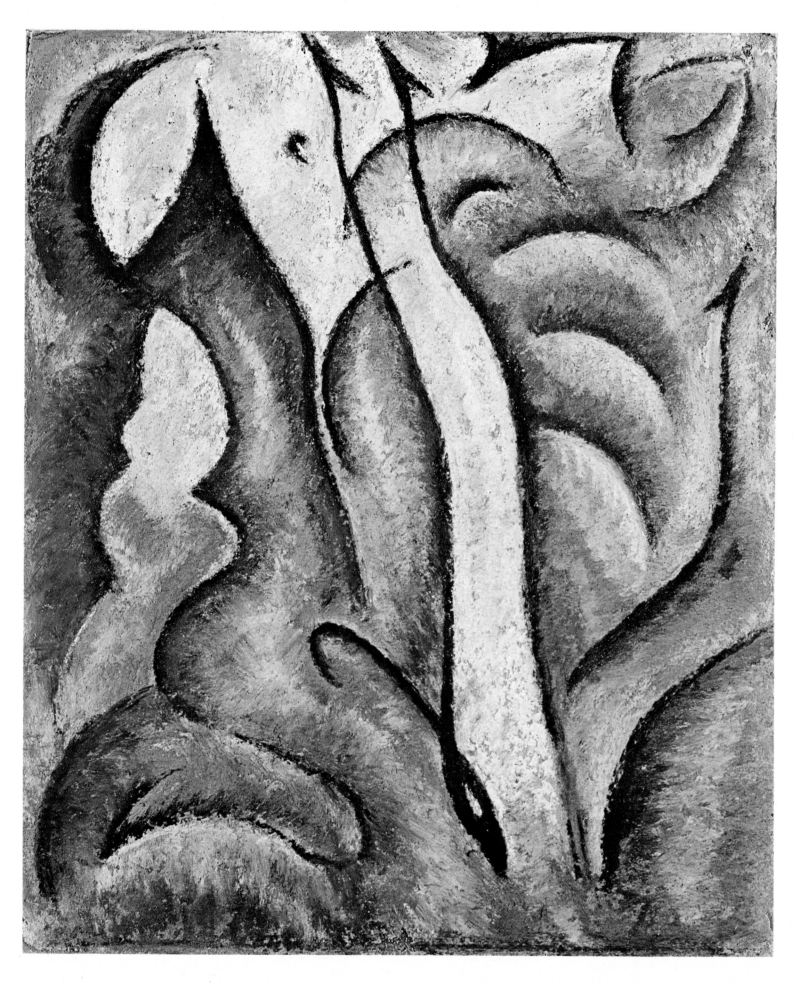

PLATE 8 ARTHUR DOVE *Sentimental Music*, 1917 (54 x 45 cm) New York, Metropolitan Museum of Art, Stieglitz Collection

PLATE 9 ARTHUR DOVE *Flour Mill Abstraction*, 1938 (66 x 40.5 cm) Washington, D. C., Phillips Collection

PLATE 10   MARSDEN HARTLEY *Portrait of a German Officer,* 1914 (173 x 105 cm) New York,
Metropolitan Museum of Art

PLATE 11   MARSDEN HARTLEY *Painting No. 4: Black Horse,* 1915 (100 x 81 cm) Philadelphia, Museum of Art, Stieglitz
Collection

PLATE 12   MARSDEN HARTLEY *The Fishermen's Last Supper,* 1940–41 (76 x 104 cm) New York, Collection of Roy R. Neuberger

PLATE 13   ALFRED MAURER *Twin Heads,* c. 1930 (67 x 46 cm) New York, Whitney Museum of American Art (Gift of Mr. and Mrs. Hudson D. Walker)

PLATE 14 MAX WEBER *Chinese Restaurant,* 1915 (102 x 122 cm) New York, Whitney Museum of American Art

PLATE 15   GEORGIA O'KEEFFE *Cow's Skull: Red, White, and Blue*, 1931 (101 x 91 cm)
New York, Metropolitan Museum of Art, Stieglitz Collection

33

Post-Armory Show Experimentation: American Cubism, Precisionism, and Synchronism

PLATE 16   OSCAR BLUEMNER *Red Glare*, 1929 (60 x 76 cm) Location Unknown

PLATE 17   WALT KUHN *The Blue Clown*, 1931 (76 x 63 cm) New York, Whitney Museum of American Art

PLATE 18   JOSEPH STELLA *The Brooklyn Bridge: Variation on an Old Theme*, 1939 (178 x 107 cm)
New York, Whitney Museum of American Art

PLATE 19 PATRICK HENRY BRUCE *Composition II*, 1918 (97 x 129.5 cm) New Haven, Yale University Art Gallery, Société Anonyme
Collection

PLATE 20   STANTON MACDONALD-WRIGHT *"Oriental." Synchromy in Blue-Green*, 1918 (92 x 127 cm) New York, Whitney Museum of American Art

PLATE 21   Morgan Russell *Four Part Synchromy, Number 7*, 1914–15 (39 x 30 cm) New York, Whitney Museum of
American Art

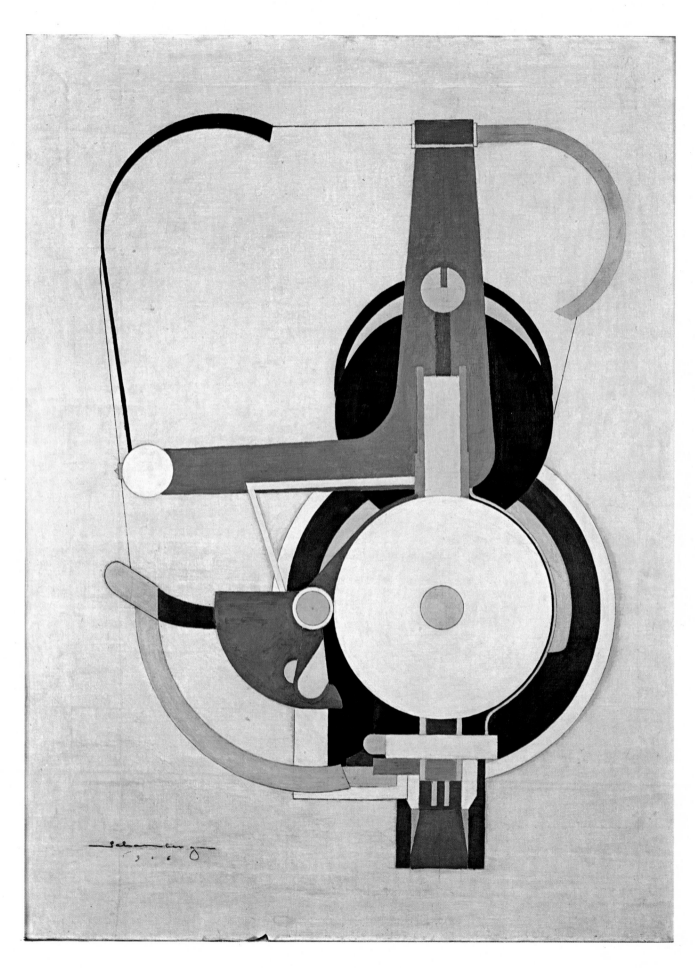

PLATE 22 MORTON SCHAMBERG *Machine,* 1916 (77 x 58 cm) New Haven, Yale University Art Gallery, Société Anonyme Collection

40

PLATE 23   ARTHUR BEECHER CARLES *Abstraction,* c. 1935 (96 x 129 cm) Philadelphia, Museum of Art (Gift of Mr. and Mrs. R. Sturgis
    Ingersoll)

PLATE 24   MARCEL DUCHAMP *The Bride,* 1912 (89.5 x 55 cm) Philadelphia, Museum of Art, Louise and Walter Arensberg Collection

PLATE 25   ARTHUR BOWEN DAVIES *Intermezzo*, 1913 (71 x 36 cm) New York,
Graham Gallery

PLATE 26   CHARLES SHEELER *Upper Deck*, 1929 (75 x 56 cm) Cambridge, Massachusetts, Fogg Art Museum (Louise E. Bettens Fund)

PLATE 27   CHARLES SHEELER *River Rouge Plant*, 1932 (51 x 61 cm) New York, Whitney Museum of American Art

PLATE 28   CHARLES DEMUTH *My Egypt,* 1927 (90 x 76 cm) New York, Whitney Museum of American Art

The Thirties: American Scene, Social Protest, Realism, Magic Realism, and Abstraction

PLATE 29   THOMAS HART BENTON *City Activities*, 1930 (230 x 340 cm) New York, New School for Social Research

PLATE 30 KENNETH HAYES MILLER *Box Party*, 1936 (152 x 117 cm) New York, Whitney Museum of
American Art (Photo: Sandak)

PLATE 31   JOHN STEUART CURRY *Baptism in Kansas*, 1928 (102 x 127 cm) New York, Whitney Museum of American Art

PLATE 32 CHARLES BURCHFIELD *House of Mystery*, 1924 (75 x 62 cm) Chicago, Art Institute of Chicago

PLATE 33   CHARLES BURCHFIELD *Church Bells Ringing, Rainy Winter Night*, 1917 (76 x 48 cm) Cleveland, Ohio, Cleveland Museum of Art (Gift of Mrs. Louise M. Dunn)

PLATE 34 EDWARD HOPPER *Early Sunday Morning,* 1930 (89 x 152 cm) New York, Whitney Museum of American Art

PLATE 35   BEN SHAHN *The Passion of Sacco and Vanzetti*, 1931–32 (215 x 122 cm) New
York, Whitney Museum of American Art

54

PLATE 37   YASUO KUNIYOSHI *Child*, 1923 (76 x 61 cm) New York, Whitney Museum of American Art (Gift of
Edith Gregor Halpert)

PLATE 36   IVAN ALBRIGHT *That Which I Should Have Done I Did Not Do*, 1931–41 (246.5 x 91.5 cm) Chicago,
Art Institute of Chicago

PLATE 38   STUART DAVIS *Lucky Strike,* 1921 (84 x 46 cm) New York, Museum of Modern Art
(Gift of The American Tobacco Company, Inc.)

PLATE 39   MORRIS GRAVES *Little Known Bird of the Inner Eye,* 1941 (52 x 92 cm) New York, Museum of Modern Art

PLATE 40   JACK LEVINE *The Feast of Pure Reason,* 1937 (106.5 x 122 cm) New York, Museum of Modern Art (Extended loan from the
United States WPA Art Program)

An American Art Emerging:
The Later Thirties and Early Forties

PLATE 41   JOSEF ALBERS *The Gate*, 1936 (47.5 x 52.5 cm) New Haven, Yale University Art Gallery, Société Anonyme
Collection

PLATE 42 STUART DAVIS *Swing Landscape*, 1938 (217 x 441 cm) Bloomington, Indiana University Art Museum

PLATE 44   GEORGE McNEIL *Green Forms Dominant*, 1938–39 (51 x 61 cm) New York, Collection of the Artist

PLATE 45   JOHN GRAHAM *Two Sisters*, 1944 (121 x 122 cm) New York, Museum of Modern Art

PLATE 46   ADOLPH GOTTLIEB *Sundeck,* 1936, College Park, University of Maryland Art Gallery, WPA Federal Art Project Collection

PLATE 47   MILTON AVERY *Young Artist*, 1943 (100 x 75 cm) New York, Collection of Roy R. Neuberger

PLATE 48   ARSHILE GORKY *The Artist and His Mother*, 1926–29 (152 x 127 cm) New York, Whitney Museum of American
Art (Gift of Julien Levy)

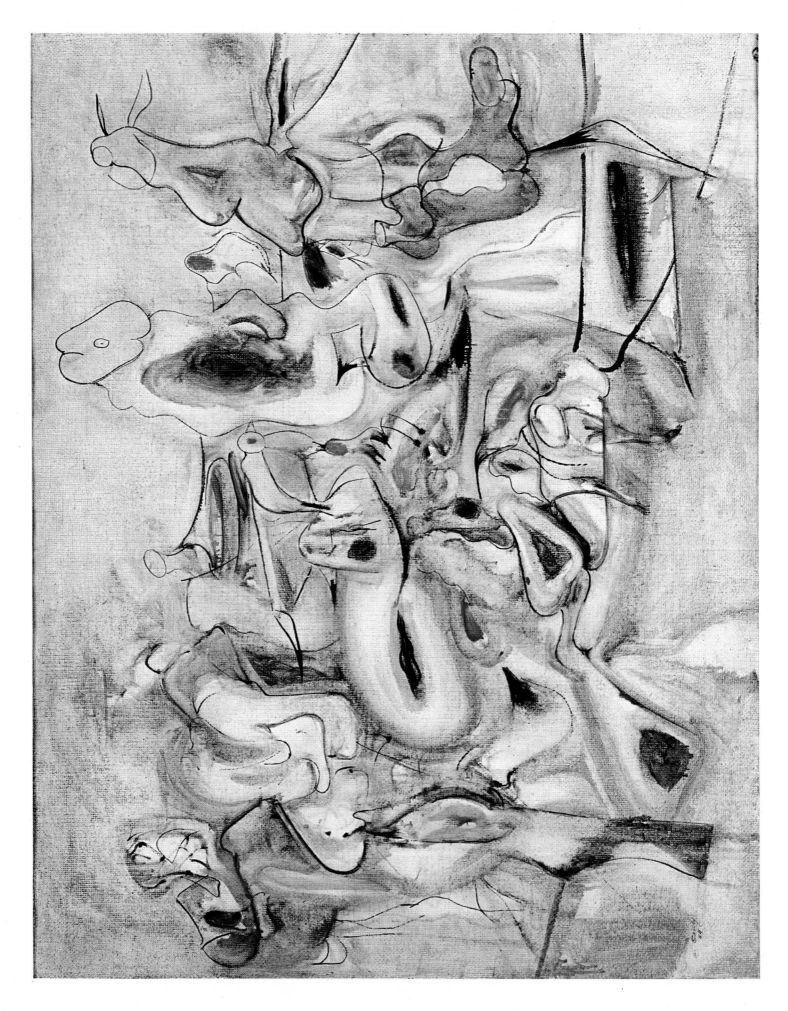

PLATE 50 ARSHILE GORKY *Good Morning, Mrs. Lincoln,* 1944 (76 x 96 cm) Paris, Private Collection

PLATE 51   ARSHILE GORKY *Painting*, 1944 (167 x 177 cm) Venice, Collection of Peggy Guggenheim

PLATE 52   WILLEM DE KOONING *Glazier,* c. 1940 (135 x 110 cm) Private Collection

PLATE 53   WILLEM DE KOONING *Two Men Standing*, c. 1938 (155.5 x 114.5 cm) Private Collection

PLATE 54   WILLEM DE KOONING *Elegy,* c. 1939 (102 x 121 cm) Private Collection

PLATE 55   AD REINHARDT *Abstract Painting,* 1938 (41 x 51 cm) New York, Estate of Ad Reinhardt

PLATE 56   MARK ROTHKO *Vessel of Magic,* c. 1946 (98.5 x 65.5 cm) New York, Brooklyn Museum

PLATE 57   MARK TOBEY *Cirque d'hiver*, 1933 (42 x 54 cm) Seattle, Collection of Mr. and Mrs. Windsor Utley

PLATE 58   JACKSON POLLOCK *Male and Female*, 1942 (180 x 120 cm) Haverford, Pennsylvania, Collection
of Mrs. H. Gates Lloyd

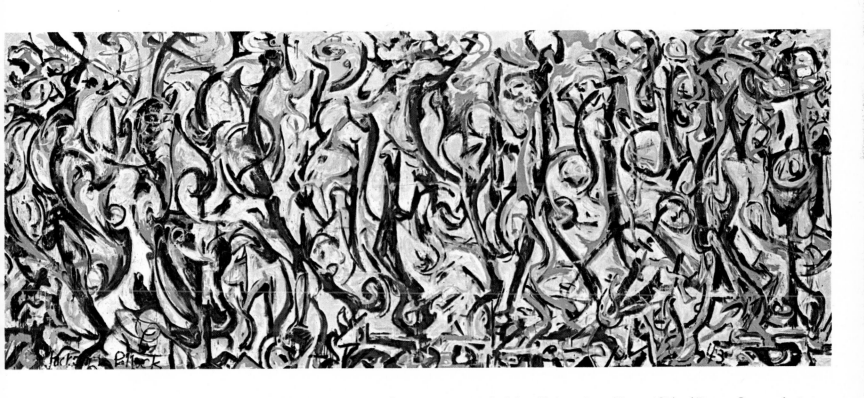

PLATE 59   JACKSON POLLOCK *Mural,* 1943 (250 x 600 cm) Iowa City, Iowa, School of Art, University of Iowa (Gift of Peggy Guggenheim)

PLATE 60   JACKSON POLLOCK *Gothic*, 1944 (210 x 140 cm) New York, Estate of the Artist

THE ARTISTS

JOSEF ALBERS

Born in 1888 in Bottrop, Germany. H[e studied at] the Royal Art School in Berlin (1913[...], and at] the School of Applied Art in Essen (19[...]) where he did his first lithography and woodcutting, expressionistic works in the manner of Hechel or Schmidt-Rotluff. He also studied at the Art Academy in Munich (1920) and at the Bauhaus in Dessau (1923), later teaching there himself until he emigrated to the United States and became director of the art department at Black Mountain College (until 1949).

As a student Albers was involved in the production and design of stained-glass windows, and later he designed furniture, creating the first bent laminated chair intended for mass production, using durable materials and a smooth, simple design he advocated in his teachings and in his own works. His aesthetic position is expressed in the statement, "In producing art I please myself and educate others to see." His own work has moved from a series of masonite paintings done from 1928–48, involving exhaustive, precise investigation of geometric forms, to his famed *Homage to the Square* paintings and prints with concentric ranges of subtly colored squares. He now lives in Hamden, Connecticut.

GEORGE WESLEY BELLOWS

Born in 1882 in Columbus, Ohio. Unlike many of his fellow artists, he never traveled outside America, but through international exhibitions and teachers like Robert Henri he was somewhat influenced by the art of Europe. In 1909, after studying painting, he set up a studio in New York near the Athletic Club in order to be close to the prizefights, which were his favorite subject. His sense of humor, slightly satirical, enlivened his views of everyday life in the city. In 1910 he exhibited along with The Eight in the Salon des Indépendants.

His expressive and dramatic drawing style was well suited to the lithographs he began after 1916. The Armory Show of 1913 had forced him to reconsider the flashy surface effects that he had used in his previous paintings. His most familiar paintings are those that depict the ringside excitement of boxers in the midst of their energetic bouts. But Bellows used many more subjects than sports activities, and in these, rather than generalize the expressions of the figures as he did in the boxing paintings, he emphasized with great sensitivity the particularities of the personality. He died in 1925 in New York.

THOMAS HART BENTON

Born in 1889, in Neosho, Missouri. Benton's father was a member of Congress, and therefore Thomas had the opportunity to be exposed to art collections in the museums of Washington while still young. At home in Missouri he illustrated and cartooned for a newspaper. He studied in Paris (1908–11) when such revolutionary modern movements as Cubism, Fauvism, and Expressionism

ALBERS *Glove Hangers*, 1928–31, Collection of the Artist

were brewing, affecting those expatriates from America who were there, as well as other native artists. But Benton returned to America only to reject this early experience with modernism. He retained his strongest impressions from the work of the Spanish painter El Greco, rather than from that of the French Modernists.

Traveling around the United States after World War I, he accrued many sketches of rural inhabitants at work and at home. During the thirties he taught at the Art Students League and became an outspoken advocate of American Scene painting, in which he employed these rural scenes and domestic themes, both in defense of his native roots and as a kind of isolationist political propaganda. During this period he was known for his semihistorical, allegorical murals, which drew their expressionistic sources from painters like El Greco or from the Mexican muralists like Orozco and Rivera. Benton lives in Kansas City, Missouri.

OSCAR F. BLUEMNER

Born in 1867 in Hanover, Germany. He came to America in 1892, having been trained as an architect and portrait painter. He was a member of Stieglitz's 291 Gallery and exhibited in the Armory Show in 1913, in the Forum Exhibition in 1916, and in many other group shows thereafter.

Influenced by both Cubism and the high color of Matisse and Fauvism, Bluemner is best known for his irrationally expressionistic use of color. As a precedent, he looked to Byzantine mosaics, Oriental art, stained glass, and manuscript illumination, and to the scientific color principles explored by Delaunay and the American Synchronists. Like Benton, he rejected abstraction as too intellectual or abstruse. His alliance was with more instinctively lyrical, emotional painters like Dove, Hartley, and O'Keeffe. Geometric landscapes, daringly colored in deep vermilions, chrome yellows, and grays, with sharp tonal variations, were characteristic of his repertoire. Stagelike lighting heightened the dramatic effect of these works, and visionary distortions also enlivened the pictures. He committed suicide in 1938, despondent at the difficulty of earning a living through his art, and discouraged by his failing eyesight.

CHARLES BURCHFIELD

Born in 1893 in Astabula Harbor, Ohio. He studied at the Cleveland School of Art in 1912, and, after serving in World War I, he worked as a wallpaper designer until 1929. In 1917 he had executed a series of pen drawings called *Conventions for Abstract Thought*. He was always concerned with moods—danger, gloom, and brooding, for example—even in his more conservative works between 1920 and 1940, during which time he recorded the small barren towns and oppressive seasonal changes in rural Ohio. More emotionally involved with his subjects than his contemporary Edward Hopper, and less politically oriented than other Regionalists, Burchfield imbued his windy rainswept streets and spooky church steeples at midnight with an almost anthropomorphic spirit.

After 1940 he went back to an earlier style, often reworking old paintings. He turned away from his familiar houses and buildings to look more closely at nature's basic shapes and mysterious forces. Watercolors were particularly well suited to his aim of capturing fleeting moods and sensations in his romantic vision of American scenes. He died in Buffalo, New York, in 1967.

JOHN STEUART CURRY

Born in 1897 in Dunavent, Kansas, and raised on a Kansas stock farm. Surprisingly enough, he was encouraged by his mother to draw, and later to study at the Art Institute in Kansas City. His work at the Art Institute of Chicago completed his formal education in art. He worked for five years as an illustrator, then traveled to Paris for a year. By the thirties, Curry had joined forces with the other rurally concerned American Scene painters, Thomas Hart Benton and Grant Wood. From 1936 until he died, he taught at the University of Wisconsin, promoting Regionalist painting and stressing the individualistic approach that he believed to be the most reliable root for all art and expression. His most famous and powerful achievements are the murals he painted during the thirties under government programs supporting the artists (W.P.A.). He depicted the people of the plains and farms he knew so well, performing their daily activities in fields, churches, and homes. He died in 1946.

ARTHUR B. DAVIES

Born in 1862 in Utica, New York, and studied at the Chicago Academy of Design. He had previously been impressed by the paintings of George Inness and Winslow Homer. After drafting as a civil engineer in Mexico in 1880, he studied at the Art Institute of Chicago for several years, and in 1886 he moved to New York. He went to the Art Students League, and he earned a living doing magazine illustrations. In 1893 an art patron was willing to send Davies to Europe, where the young artist saw works by the Venetians, the Pre-Raphaelites, Whistler, Puvis de Chavannes, and the German Romantics. Early paintings display some of these influences with their dreamy pastoral scenes and rich, heavily textured color.

Davis first exhibited with The Eight—Robert Henri, John Sloan, and others known as the Ashcan School of New York Realists—at the Macbeth Gallery in 1908. In 1913 he was elected president of the Association of American Painters and Sculptors, and shortly thereafter he was chosen to head the organization of the Armory Show. He seemed to represent a median figure between Henri, the more academic painters, and the avant-garde. He was acquainted with wealthy collectors like Lillie Bliss. He and Walt Kuhn assembled works for the show by traveling throughout Europe, scouring Paris, Germany, and England for modern paintings. He died in 1928, in Florence, Italy.

STUART DAVIS

Born in 1894 in Philadelphia, Pennsylvania. Davis's father, art editor of the Philadelphia *Press*, employed Glackens, Sloan, Luks, and Henri, introducing them to his son Stuart, who was earn-

BURCHFIELD
Street Light Shining Through Rain and Fog, 1917

ing his living by the age of nineteen doing cartoons and illustrations. In 1916–17 he exhibited at the Independents Exhibition, and as early as 1917 he had attempted Cubist-derived abstractions, though he consistently described himself as a Realist. Following the example of Henri, Davis sketched the life of the streets, its signs,

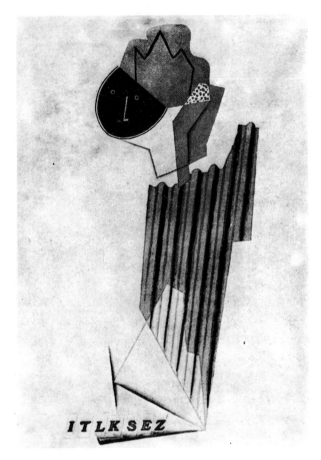

Davis *ITLKSEZ*, 1921

people, places, colors, shapes, and music. The Armory Show of 1913 made a great impression on him, and he was especially influenced by the decorative color and formal generalizations of Gauguin, van Gogh, and Matisse. His first one-man show was at the Newark Museum in 1925, and in 1927 Edith Gregor Halpert of the Downtown Gallery became his permanent dealer. From 1931–32 he taught at the Art Students League, and the next year Davis enrolled in the W.P.A./F.A.P., working as a mural painter. He headed the Artists Union and was active during the thirties in the maintenance and insurance of artists' rights while working under government auspices. In 1935 he was editor of *Art Front*, the publication of the Artists Union. In the decade between 1940 and 1950 he taught again, this time at New York's progressive New School, and in 1945 the Museum of Modern Art gave him a retrospective exhibition, followed in 1957 by a similar showing at both the Walker Art Center in Minneapolis and at the Whitney Museum in New York. He painted actively until his death in 1964 in New York.

WILLEM DE KOONING

Born in Rotterdam in 1904, and first educated in his native Holland. He worked for a firm of commercial artists who gave him a strong background in fine and applied arts, crafts' techniques, and classical academic discipline. For several years he worked under a sign and display painter, Bernard Romein, from whom de Kooning gained a background in traditional methods, as well as an acquaintance with the vanguard movements such as the de Stijl group in Holland and the revolutionaries working in Paris. After a stay in Belgium painting and working, he returned to Rotterdam and to classes at its Academy. In 1926 he came to the United States and first supported himself as a house painter in Hoboken, New Jersey, before moving permanently to New York. Early work from about 1928 indicates experimental abstraction referring to Kandinsky's geometric works. In 1933 he became friendly with Arshile Gorky, with whom he shared a studio during the late thirties. Mutual influences and experiences reinforced their painting. Both drew extensively from their admiration for and interest in Picasso, Cubism, Ingres, Miró, Kandinsky, and Stuart Davis.

De Kooning was supported as a full-time painter for the first time in his life by the W.P.A. Federal Arts Project. He worked for it in 1935, on a mural for the Williamsburg Housing Project (never executed, however), and assisted Léger on another unexecuted mural designed for the French Lines' Pier in New York. In 1948, in his first New York one-man show at the Charles Egan Gallery, he exhibited a series of masterful black and white abstract canvases. In the summer of 1958 de Kooning taught at Black Mountain

Photograph of Willem de Kooning in his studio

College, renewing his acquaintance with Albers and the designer-engineer Buckminster Fuller. He also taught briefly at Yale in 1950–51. After a period of broad, colorful abstractions based on landscape, he was to stick to the female motif well into the sixties, in hundreds of oil paintings, drawings, and gouaches, with more frequent shows at the Janis Gallery in 1953, at the Martha Jackson Gallery in 1955, again at the Janis Gallery in 1956 and 1959, and a large, climactic showing at the Museum of Modern Art in 1969.

DEMUTH *I Saw the Figure 5 in Gold,* 1928, New York, Metropolitan Museum of Art, Stieglitz Collection

CHARLES DEMUTH

Born in 1883 in Lancaster, Pennsylvania. Demuth took up art at an early age. He studied at Franklin and Marshall College, Drexel Institute of Technology, the Pennsylvania Academy of Fine Arts (1905–1908, with Thomas Anschutz), and at the Académie Julian in Paris from 1912 to 1914. His exposure to Cubism in Paris provided him with a means to become one of America's first modernist experimenters.

Because he never had to struggle for a living, he was not as embittered by the battle for recognition as were many of his contemporaries. His paintings sold moderately well, and he had his first one-man show in 1915 at the Daniels Gallery in New York, later joining Stieglitz's artists, showing with them in exhibits at the Intimate Gallery from 1926 to 1929, at An American Place in 1931, and after 1931 at Edith Gregor Halpert's Downtown Gallery. In 1949 a retrospective of his work was held at the Museum of Modern Art. Watercolor was his favorite medium, well suited to his exquisiteness of taste, delicacy of perception, and tendency to work on an intimate scale. He loved theater and dance-hall spectacles, and his

paintings and book illustrations of these themes are often reflective of the decadence that accompanied the more lighthearted aspects of theatrical life. The contortions of figures and the more perverse and ironic book illustrations are evidence of an underlying disquiet in the artist's personality and perhaps, like Toulouse Lautrec (who was lame like Demuth), he felt a peculiar empathy with the discomfort of his subjects. Demuth died in 1935.

ARTHUR DOVE

Born in 1880 in New York. His important formative influences can be traced to his hardworking English-American parents, who brought Dove up on a farm in New York State; Newton Weatherly, a neighboring vegetable farmer who painted and encouraged Dove to paint at an early age, was also a significant influence. Dove supported himself for many difficult years as a farmer. He was a successful illustrator, and he was perhaps one of the first Americans to do nonrepresentational pictures around 1910, paralleling Kandinsky's improvisations of the same period. In that same year, Dove participated in a show at Stieglitz's 291 Gallery with Weber, Hartley, and Carles, and he was a close friend of another of Stieglitz's protégés, Alfred Maurer. In Paris in 1908, Dove was impressed by the Fauvist paintings at the Salon d'Automne. When he returned home, he painted his "extractions" from nature, condensed motifs that aimed to symbolize the forces and energies of natural life. Dove's later paintings still contain some kind of recognizable imagery, and during the late thirties he expressed his ambition "to take wind and water and sand as a motif and work with them...simplified in most cases to color and force lines and substances, just as music has done with sound." He died in 1946 in New York.

WILLIAM GLACKENS

Born in 1870 in Philadelphia and studied art at the Pennsylvania Academy of Fine Arts. He then worked as an illustrator for the Philadelphia *Press.* In 1891 he met Robert Henri—a decisive event in his life—for Henri was to encourage the young illustrator to take up oil painting. Together with Everett Shinn, George Luks, and John Sloan, all on the staff of the same journal, Glackens formed a group that met frequently at Henri's studio. He eventually became a member of The Eight, who exhibited their realistic paintings at the Macbeth Gallery in 1908 in New York. In 1895 Glackens went to Paris, where he exhibited at the official Salon. The show of The Eight in 1908 declared the independence of his colleagues and himself from the tastes and system controlled by the academic establishment. The manner of Impressionist painter Renoir strongly influenced his later work, with its luminous, charming nudes and female portraits, its patchwork of tiny strokes, and scintillation of blushing red, green, orange, and yellow flecks of color. For years Glackens was the consultant to collector Dr. Albert C. Barnes, a childhood friend. Glackens died in 1938 in New York.

ARSHILE GORKY

Born in 1904 in Khorkhom, Armenia. The rich folk tradition of Armenia was to influence Gorky's later creativity considerably. He came to America with his sister in 1920 and lived in Boston and Providence, where he attended art classes at the Rhode Island School of Design, Providence Technical High School, and New School of Design in Boston. In 1925 he changed his name from Vosdanig Manoog Adoian to Arshile Gorky and began to study at New York's Grand Central School, where he also taught until 1931. He met Stuart Davis, and in 1933 he became very friendly with de Kooning. In 1933 three of his still lifes were exhibited in the Museum of Modern Art's exhibition of younger artists. The Whitney Museum then purchased a painting, and four years later his first one-man show occurred at the Mellon Galleries in Philadelphia; in 1941 a retrospective of twenty paintings was held at the San Francisco Museum of Art, and from 1945 to 1948 he exhibited at the Julien Levy Gallery in New York. In 1935 Gorky was employed by the W.P.A. to paint murals, producing one for Newark Airport, and later another for the World's Fair Aviation Building (1939). In 1942 the Museum of Modern Art acquired one of his finer works, *Garden in Sochi*, and in 1946 he appeared in the Museum of Modern Art's 14 Americans show. In 1944 he met André Breton and the Surrealists, who were to influence his thinking and work. In 1946 twenty-seven paintings were burned in his studio, and he underwent an operation for cancer; in 1947 he moved to the country with his wife, and two years later his neck was broken and his painting arm injured in a car accident. Personal problems and years of intense emotional strain and disappointment proved too much for him, and he hanged himself on July 21, 1948.

MARSDEN HARTLEY

Born in 1877 in Lewiston, Maine, he claimed himself a "Maine-iac" to the last. His art education began in 1892 in Cleveland, then continued at the Chase School in New York under Frank Vincent DuMond, followed by a year under Edwin Blashfield at the National Academy of Design. By 1908 he was painting in an Impressionistic landscape style, and the next year he had a one-man exhibition at Stieglitz's 291 Gallery. In 1910 he met Albert Pinkham Ryder, and in 1912 Stieglitz, assisted by Arthur B. Davies, financed Hartley's trip to Paris and Berlin, where he saw works of Cézanne and Picasso. In 1913 he did improvisational paintings based on ideas about the spiritual harmony of geometrical forms, and in 1914 some of his works done in Paris and Berlin were exhibited at 291. In the Forum Exhibition of 1916 his Kandinsky-like paintings of 1913 were shown, and in 1916–17 he also did some paintings on glass, stimulated by an interest in native folk artists' techniques.

In 1918 he went to Taos and Santa Fe, New Mexico, and in 1922 he was again in Berlin. Hartley was also a poet and often used the mountain slope as a recurring theme in later landscapes. By

Photograph of Arshile Gorky, 1933

HARTLEY *Military Symbols, 2,* 1913–14, New York, Metropolitan Museum of Art (Rogers Fund)

1937, after working on Symbolist nature paintings and after briefly working for the W.P.A., he exhibited stormy landscapes, woods, and winter scenes at An American Place Gallery.

He died in 1943 in Ellsworth, Maine, having painted over one thousand pictures and published four books.

ROBERT HENRI

Born in 1865 in Cincinnati. His traditional training in art started at the Pennsylvania Academy of Fine Arts, then continued at the Académie Julian and the École des Beaux-Arts in Paris. Settling in Philadelphia in 1891, he came into contact with illustrators Glackens, Luks, Sloan, and Shinn. He became their mentor and friend, and, after a trip to Europe in 1901, he introduced them to the works of the European masters who influenced his own painting—Manet, Velázquez, Hals, Courbet, and Goya.

After 1901 Henri moved to New York with his group of friends and taught at the William Merritt Chase School. Discouraged by the traditionalism of Chase, Henri opened his own school to foster his ideas about individualism for the artist. He battled against the stuffiness of Victorian conservative tastes, appealing to his students—who included Stuart Davis, Rockwell Kent, Edward Hopper, Yasuo Kuniyoshi, George Bellows, and Morgan Russell—to look directly to life for models, rather than to European prototypes. His teaching inspired this whole generation of artists to break away from canons of accepted taste and establishment approval. Henri helped to organize the 1908 exhibition of The Eight, as well as the 1910 Independents Exhibition. He died in 1929 in New York.

HANS HOFMANN

Born in 1880 in Weissenburg, Bavaria, Germany. As a child he was exposed to the arts; he played music, drew, and developed a love for nature. In 1896 he left home and worked in the mechanical and scientific field but soon enrolled in art school. In 1903 he met Phillip Freudenberg, the patron who subsidized Hofmann's years in Paris until 1914. In 1904 he studied at the École de la Grande Chaumière and became active in the international artists' circles; he met the painter Delaunay and also met Picasso, Braque, Matisse, and other Cubists. At this time he was painting still lifes, landscapes, and figure studies in a Cubist style. In 1909 he showed with the Neue Sezession in Berlin, and the next year he had his first one-man show at Paul Cassirer's gallery in Berlin. Returning to Germany during World War I, Hofmann earned a living by teaching. In 1925 he opened the successful Hans Hofmann School of Fine Arts in Munich. In 1932 Hofmann was advised by his wife to close the Munich school because of government hostility toward artists and intellectuals, and he settled in America, teaching first at the Art Students League in New York. In 1933 he opened a school on Madison Avenue, and by 1934

HOFMANN *Black and Red Ribbons*

he had initiated the Hans Hofmann School of Fine Arts on Fifty-seventh Street, moving it downtown to Eighth Street in 1936, and also opening a Provincetown, Massachusetts, branch in the summer of 1935. In 1940 he moved increasingly toward abstraction, with his first New York exhibition at Peggy Guggenheim's Art of This Century Gallery, a show of abstract oils, gouaches, and drawings. A large retrospective was held in 1948 at the Addison Gallery of American Art, Andover, Massachusetts, in 1954 at the Baltimore Museum of Art, in 1957 at the Whitney Museum, in 1963 at the Santa Barbara Museum of Art, and also at the Museum of Modern Art in New York. A trip back to Paris in 1949 brought him to the studios of Braque, Picasso, and Brancusi. By 1958 Hofmann closed his New York and Provincetown schools to devote his later years entirely to painting. His philosophy and teaching inspired a broad range of painters who studied at his schools, from the older, first generation Abstract Expressionists to the younger generation who followed the example of de Kooning, Pollock, and Still. Hofmann died in 1966 in Provincetown.

EDWARD HOPPER

Born in 1882 in Nyack, New York. Although Hopper grew up in the same generation as the Ashcan School, studying with them at Henri's New York School of Art from 1900–1906, his interest in the city and in direct observation of the life around him was much more detached than the partisan pictures of Henri, Luks, Sloan, or Bellows, and less idyllic than those of Glackens, Prendergast, or Davies. In the years between 1906 and 1910, Hopper spent time in Europe, mostly in Paris. One of his paintings was included in the Armory Show in 1913, but he, along with other artists, was usually rejected by the Academy exhibitions. He supported himself by commercial art for many years. Hopper's work constituted one of the first one-man shows at the Whitney Studio Club in 1920, and during the next decade the increasing recognition brought to him by exhibitions resulted in work that was more assured, bolder in design and subject, and classic in its spareness and strength of mood. He died in 1967.

YASUO KUNIYOSHI

Born in 1893 in Okayama, Japan, and came to the United States about 1906, studying first at the Los Angeles School of Art, then in 1910 in New York with Robert Henri, from 1914–16 at the Independents School, and from 1916–20 at the Art Students League under Kenneth Hayes Miller. By 1917 he had exhibited works with the Penguin Club members, and he had his first one-man show at the Daniels Gallery in 1922, showing there until 1930 when he moved to the Downtown Gallery and exhibited there until 1953. Although trained by, and friendly with urban Realist painters like Miller, Henri, Reginald Marsh, and others, Kuniyoshi's art was more instinctive and personal from the start. His Oriental origins interested him in broad areas of white space and in the linear facility particularly evident in his lithographs. But his subject matter was the figure, animals, still-life objects, and nature. For two years during World War II, he worked for the Graphic Division under the W.P.A., designing posters. Friendly with Max Weber, Alexander Brook, Reginald Marsh, and Jacques Émile Blanche, Kuniyoshi was also influenced during the forties by the expressionistic and lyrical style of his intimate acquaintance Jules Pascin. Kuniyoshi died in 1953 in New York.

WALTER KUHN

Born in 1877 in Brooklyn, New York. Like his contemporaries Glackens, Sloan, Shinn, and Luks, Kuhn began his artistic career as a newspaper cartoonist in San Francisco, supporting himself for over ten years by his drawings. He was able to continue studies in art in both Paris and Munich (1901), also traveling through Holland, Germany, Spain, and Italy. Selected to aid Arthur B. Davies in the organization and selection of the Armory Show of 1913, he helped to gather the finest examples of European Modernism—Cubism, Fauvism, Expressionism, Symbolism, and nineteenth-century precedents—as well as examples by those painters in America who had begun to adopt modernist techniques. Kuhn loved the world of the circus as well as that of the theater, and he painted many half-length and frontal portraits of the characters who populated these spectacles. He died in 1949 in New York.

GEORGE LUKS

Born in 1867 in Williamsport, Pennsylvania. He studied art at the Pennsylvania Academy of Fine Arts, then worked in Düsseldorf and Paris; he stayed in Europe for ten years, concentrating on drawing rather than painting. In 1895 he came back to America to work as an illustrator on the Philadelphia *Press,* where he became acquainted with Sloan, Glackens, Shinn, and, later, Henri. He and Glackens were employed by the *Evening Bulletin* to cover the Spanish-American War. He also worked as a cartoonist for the New York *World.*

Henri influenced him to look to New York's street life for themes that he could paint in oil, and, extending the vitality and humor of his illustrations, Luks favored street urchins, coal miners, and wrestlers as subjects for his work. He also looked to Franz Hals, his favorite Dutch master, for stylistic guidance. His temperament was well suited to the battles against academic constraint that Henri, The Eight, and other contemporary artists had to wage. Luks died in 1933 in New York.

STANTON MacDONALD-WRIGHT

Born in 1890 in Charlottesville, Virginia. Stanton began taking painting lessons after his family moved to California. In 1905 he enrolled at the Los Angeles Art Students League, where he worked under Warren T. Hedges. At seventeen MacDonald-Wright left for Paris, and for six months he studied at the École des Beaux-Arts, the Académie Julian, and the Académie Colarossi, and became interested in Cézanne's watercolors at this time. He also began to study the pointillist Post-Impressionism of Seurat and Paul Signac. By 1910–12, assimilating these influences, he became interested in scientific color theory. In 1911, in Paris, he met the American painter Morgan Russell, who knew the "orphic" Cubist Robert Delaunay and who was himself concerned with color theory. Officially joining forces with Russell for two audacious exhibitions in 1913—at the Neue Kunstsalon in Munich and the Galerie Bernheim Jeune in Paris—the two issued a manifesto in which they stated their program to apply scientific color principles to a new vision of pictorial space and organization. Returning to the United States in 1913, MacDonald-Wright arranged another joint exhibi-

KUNIYOSHI *Little Joe with Cow,* 1923, Collection of Edith Gregor Halpert

tion at the Carroll Galleries in New York, and in 1916 he participated in the Forum exhibition, showing works that gave evidence of the more successful results obtained since the first 1913 exhibitions. In 1917 he exhibited at Stieglitz's 291 Gallery, and in the next year at the Daniels Gallery. Poor health prompted him to move to California that year, and, after 1920, he abandoned the exploration of Synchromist abstraction. For forty years thereafter, he sought bases for color painting, and finally, in 1954, he returned to abstraction. He now lives in Pacific Palisades, California.

JOHN MARIN

Born in 1870 in Rutherford, New Jersey, and spent several years of apprenticeship as an architect. In 1899 he was sent to the Pennsylvania Academy of Fine Arts by his family. There, students split camps between the models of Whistler and John Singer Sargent. In 1904 he attended the Art Students League, and then, at the age of thirty-five, he went to Paris to spend five years studying and painting. In 1909 he exhibited with Alfred Maurer at Stieglitz's 291 Gallery, and in 1911 he first saw Cézanne's paintings there, which were to serve as a model for his development of an elliptical, allusive watercolor style for his transcriptions of the scenes and architecture of Manhattan and, later, the coastal landscapes of Maine. Close to Stieglitz, Marin was loyally supported by the dealer throughout his career, and much of this patron's skill was put to the promotion of Marin's work. Marin died in 1953 in Cape Split, Maine.

GEORGIA O'KEEFFE

Born in 1887 in Sun Prairie, Wisconsin. She studied at the Art Institute of Chicago from 1904 to 1905, with William Merritt Chase in 1907 and 1908, and with Arthur Wesley Dow at Columbia University in 1916. In that same year her delicate charcoal drawings were shown to Stieglitz, who was impressed by their sensitivity and by the fact that they were done by a woman. He exhibited these

O'KEEFFE *Blue, No. IV,* 1916

(against her initial objections), and O'Keeffe later became his wife, as well as the inspiration for some of his finest photographs and one of the major figures in his gallery promotions. O'Keeffe rebelled against her earlier traditional training with Chase and developed an extremely personal vocabulary in her art. Shows of her work were held at the 291 Gallery in 1917, at the Intimate Gallery in 1927 and 1929, at An American Place in 1931, and from 1937 to 1961, at Edith Gregor Halpert's Downtown Gallery. In 1946 the Museum of Modern Art had a retrospective of her paintings. An independent female, O'Keeffe's work stands as the evidence of a mature aesthetic who developed with little outside influence during a long career. She lives in Abiquiu, New Mexico.

CHARLES SHEELER

Born in 1883 in Philadelphia, Pennsylvania, and was enrolled in the School of Industrial Art from 1900 to 1903. He later studied at the Pennsylvania Academy of Fine Arts with Chase, and then went to Europe to see the works of the old masters. For a long time Sheeler shared a studio with Morton Schamberg, who had studied architecture and later had brought Sheeler into contact with Walter Arensberg's circle of avant-garde artistic and literary friends. In 1908, in Italy, he was especially impressed by such Italian Renaissance painters as Piero della Francesca. Paris introduced him to the work of the moderns—Cézanne, Picasso, Braque, and Matisse—and the beginnings of Cubism that he witnessed there finally forced him to abandon the Chase manner. In 1912, both he and his friend Schamberg took up commercial photography as a livelihood. He participated in

MARIN *The Woolworth Building, No. 31,* 1912, Collection of Eugene Meyer

the Armory Show and in the Forum Exhibition of 1916, as well as the Independents Exhibition of 1917. A friend of the writer and dealer Marius de Zayas, Sheeler showed some early photographs at his gallery in 1915.

Dividing his time between New York and commercial schedules photographing for *Vogue, Vanity Fair,* and other publications, by 1923 Sheeler had achieved some amount of recognition. His photographs often remained on a higher level artistically than his later paintings. In 1939 a retrospective of his work was held at the Museum of Modern Art in New York, and in 1968 another appeared at the Whitney Museum. He died in 1965.

JOHN SLOAN

Born in 1871 in Lock Haven, Pennsylvania. A colleague of Luks, Shinn, and Glackens, Sloan illustrated for the Philadelphia *Press,* and was introduced to Henri, who encouraged him to paint in oil after 1897. In 1904 he went to New York along with his friends, and in 1908 he exhibited with them as The Eight. Sloan developed a visual shorthand to record spontaneously the sensational events and picturesque details of city life. In 1919 he went to Santa Fe, New Mexico, a trip that stimulated a fruitful series of works in later years. He was the only member of The Eight who never studied in Europe. New York City was Sloan's great passion and inspiration.

Elected director of the Art Students League in 1931, Sloan perpetuated Henri's viewpoint there for many years. He struggled to understand the concepts of Modernism exposed to him by the Armory Show, but he generally dismissed Impressionism and Post-Impressionism as superficial "eyesight" painting. His realistic cityscapes of the rivers, ferries, bridges, and buildings of New York were freshly graphic, and his sense of color was subtly combined with the superimposed linear network that he used increasingly after 1929 when he began to use glazes of tempera over oil. In 1950 the Whitney Museum held a retrospective of his work. He died in 1951 in Hanover, New Hampshire.

MAX WEBER

Born in 1881 in Byelostok, in Russia. At the age of ten he came to America and settled in Brooklyn, New York. From 1898 to 1900 he studied theory and design at Pratt Institute under Arthur Wesley Dow. In 1905 he went to Paris and studied at the Académie Julian and at the Académie de la Grande Chaumière; he then traveled to Spain. Living in Paris for four years, he met Picasso, Delaunay, Gleizes, Apollinaire, and became a close friend of Henri Rousseau, whose genius Weber recognized and supported by arranging his first exhibition in 1910 at the 291 Gallery, when he returned to New York. Exhibiting with Stieglitz in 1909 and 1911, his Cubist-inspired nudes were attacked by the critics. In 1913 he participated in Roger Fry's Grafton Gallery group show, which was to serve as one of the examples for the Armory Show.

Although he admired and imitated Picasso in his early works, Weber was also very interested in African Art, which he used in order to capture a fresh perception of forms and design. When he returned to America, the most "advanced" art being produced was Henri and The Eight's quotidian genre paintings; Weber's work looked very strange to native eyes. From 1917 to 1919 he produced some small sculptures and paintings based on religious subjects. During the period between 1915 and 1923, he taught at the Art Students League and continued to make studies based on the art of aboriginal and primitive tribes, and on the Mayan, Aztec, and American Indians. After 1924 he received more recognition and participated in more exhibitions, though by this time he had returned to a Chagall-like figurative expressionism. He died in 1961.

WEBER *Rush Hour in New York,* 1915

List of Illustrations